THE
TOM WILLS
PICTURE
SHOW

Martin Flanagan

ETT IMPRINT
Exile Bay

for Ruth Brain

This edition published by ETT Imprint, Exile Bay 2018

ETT IMPRINT
PO Box R1906

Royal Exchange NSW 1225
Australia

ISBN 978-1-925416-04-6 (paper)
ISBN 978-1-925706-62-8 (ebook)

Design by Hanna Gottlieb

Tom Wills, pioneer of Australian Rules Football, 1857.

FOREWORD

In 1998, I wrote "The Call", a book recreating the life of Tom Wills. The cover said it was a novel but it wasn't really - if a novel is a bubble of adult make-believe, I kept bursting the bubble. I made an assumption about Tom Wills — that, like myself, he was a whitefeller influenced by blackfellers — but thereafter bent my imagining of him to every fact as I encountered it.

My book threatened some people because they jumped to the conclusion that I was portraying Tom Wills as a moral hero. I don't think Tom Wills was a moral hero any more than I think Ian Botham was a moral hero when he walked out on Somerset County Cricket Club after his black West Indian team-mates, Joel Garner and Viv Richards, got sacked in 1985. I don't think Botham saw himself as a champion of race politics. I think he was a great cricketer who knew two other great cricketers when he encountered them and revelling in their talents also meant embracing them as human beings. No matter how corrupt sport becomes, there is within it a radical innocence: when people play together so many barriers - cultural, racial, political - become superfluous.

Tom Wills' father Horatio was the first white settler in the Ararat region of western Victoria, arriving in the late 1830s. In 2008, however, when the AFL celebrated its 150th year, an official history was produced and an eminent place within it was given to an essay by Gillian Hibbins titled "A Seductive Myth" and sub-titled "Wills and the Aboriginal Game". Basically, her argument boiled down to the assertion that as there was no written evidence of Aboriginal football being played at Moyston, it could not be assumed that it was. For a long time it was assumed that Australian football was a colonial off-shoot of 19th century English school games. Clearly, it was heavily influenced by them, but that does not sever Tom Wills' link with Aboriginal football.

There are three things I know about Aboriginal football and Moyston.

Number one – the local Aboriginal people, the Tjapwurrung, had their own word for football: mingorm. Did the Italians invent the word macaroni without ever having seen or eaten a macaroni? Did any people in the history of the world ever invent a word for something which they didn't know to exist?

Number two – James Dawson was a Scottish squatter in the western district in the 1840s who actually liked Aboriginal people and spent a lot of time with them. His 1881 book Australian Aborigines. The Languages and Customs of Several Tribes of Aborigines in the Western District of Victoria, Australia is regarded as authoritative. Dawson describes a big corroboree at Terang and gives an elaborate and much-quoted account of the Aboriginal football he saw being played, especially the leaping and kicking. Dawson lists the Tjapwurrung as being one of the tribes present. Amy Saunders, a Koori woman with a sharp wit, satirised the argument that the Tjapwurrung didn't have a version of football thus: "Do you know what they're saying now? They're saying there was a tribe of blackfellers in Victoria who didn't like footy. Well, they must have all got killed out because there's none of them around now".

And, thirdly, the closest living person to the whole Tom Wills story is Lawton Wills Cooke, now well into his 90s and living in Melbourne. He is the grandson of Tom Wills's younger brother Horace. Horace Wills told his daughter, Lawton's mother, and Lawton's mother told him, that when Tom Wills was at Moyston he played Aboriginal football with a stuffed possum skin bound up in sinew.

In "The Call", Tom Wills is seen through the eyes of characters who knew him, all of them coming to Wills and what he represented from different directions. I provided an outline of the person I thought Tom Wills was but there was a point beyond which I wasn't prepared to go in terms of describing him more closely. I said earlier that my assumption in writing the book was that, like me, Tom Wills was a whitefeller influenced by blackfellers. What I didn't know was how deeply he had been influenced by Aboriginal culture and in exactly what ways.

I've met whitefellers who can speak Aboriginal languages; I've never met one who grew up speaking the Aboriginal language for the place he was growing up in. Tom Wills did. As I once said to a Jewish audience, speaking the Aboriginal language for the place you're from in Australia is like speaking Hebrew in Israel. Wills also knew Tjapwurrung songs and dances and there are various reports of him playing games with Aboriginal children as a child. This is surely the most believable part of the story because, at one level, his life was one long game. That's what Tom Wills was - a player.

In 2006, "The Call" was made into a play by director Bruce Myles after we co-wrote the script together. We had three Aboriginal actors, two non-Aboriginal actors and an Aboriginal dancer. When we did a reading of the script, the first question came from the Aboriginal dancer, since deceased. He said, "Did Tom go through Law?" That is – did Tom go through Law, did he do men's business, was he initiated? It's a whole dif-

3

ferent story if he was - the conflict within him would have run so much deeper. But when I wrote "The Call" I didn't speculate on such things. They were too big. They pushed the narrative too much in one direction and, at the end of the day, it would only be my imagining. I didn't want to open one door and then close another. Now, ten years later, do I think Tom Wills was initiated? I doubt it. My impression is that circumcision generally occurs around the age of 12 or 13 when boys are on the cusp of manhood by which Tom was mostly in a boarding school in Melbourne. So how far into Aboriginal culture did he go? Far enough for the Tjapwurrung elders to send a messenger to the Wills house asking when Tom was coming home after he went to the Rugby school in England. That suggests to me that the elders saw young Tom as a bridge between the cultures, one they desperately needed having become refugees in their own land.

Tom Wills was sent to Rugby at the age of 15. One, and probably both, of Tom's grandfathers were convicts. Ten years after Tom arrived at Rugby, Charles Dickens published "Great Expectations", his novel about the shame felt by an upwardly mobile young man from the lower classes of English society (helped on his way, as it turns out, by a convict transported to Australia). Anyone who has been to a boarding school can imagine how dangerous such shameful knowledge would be to a 15-year-old. From a young age, I concluded, Tom Wills, at least in his dealings with the outside world, was a person with a hidden life. On the sports field, he was the opposite - nothing was hidden. Was he aware of these opposites in his character? I doubt it. Insight into self doesn't seem to have been one of his virtues. Insight into games was another matter.

My aim in writing "The Call" was to get Tom to rise up from the unmarked grave in which his corpse was dumped to take his place in the Australian consciousness. But to really implant a story in the national psyche, you need to make either a film or a television mini-series and, in Australia, that is very difficult. Over the past 30 years, I've been party to futile attempts to "get up" films and mini-series about both Tom Wills and Weary Dunlop. In 2013, a bold trio from Sydney – David Thrum,

Tom Thompson and Phil Austin – took up the Tom Wills challenge once more. I wrote the treatment; they took it upon themselves to place it with as many people in the film and television industry as they could. The replies were uniformly depressing. There were issues of cultural politics. The ABC and people connected with government funding bodies were apprehensive about the scene involving the Cullinlaringo massacre, the biggest massacre of whites by blacks in Australian history. No matter that the script detailed that the whites then went out and killed possibly ten times as many blacks in retributive raids or through the agency of the Native Police. But the most common response was that the ending – Tom committing suicide in a horrible manner - was "too negative".

In fact, Tom's suicide isn't the ending – the final scene is Warlpiri man Liam Jurrah taking the 2010 AFL Mark of the Year, tumbling over the top of a pack and catching the ball on the way down. But that scene, and all which it implied, was routinely overlooked because of the manner of Wills's death. In 1880, Tom Wills was buried in an unmarked grave and his memory was deleted from polite society because he committed suicide. Australians in the 21st century would think themselves so much more broad-minded than that, but the reality is that it was still a story no-one wanted to tell. I understand that all sorts of modifications and additions have to be made to a historical story in bringing it to the screen, but there were issues I would not compromise on and one was the stature of the drama.

Tom Wills is the young man with at least two, and possibly four, different versions of Australian history running through his head. (blackfeller, whitefeller, convict, squatter and all the possible variations thereof). No-one in his time understood him. How could they? He didn't understand himself. All he knew was that when he was out there, on the sports field, he was himself. Out there, he did what he had always done, what had made him a great sportsman – he did what came naturally to him and that inevitably takes us back to the factors which shaped his nature. Towards the end of his life, Tom expressed the fear that there was no place for him. In one terrible sense, he was correct. He had shared the innocence of play with Aboriginal kids, he had witnessed the barbarity of the frontier war, he had coached the Aboriginal cricket team. Who had seen what he'd seen? He was the old sportsman, the former champion whose life had been filled with crowds. Now they were gone and he was alone in a haunted landscape. Tom Wills is a tragedy. What's more, he's an Australian tragedy.

In 2013, when I took on the task of writing a film treatment about Tom Wills, I crossed a personal line. What films and novels have in common is that the reader/viewer has to be able to visualise the subject — has to be able, literally, to see them in their mind's eye. And so, for four weeks, I dared myself to actually picture Tom Wills in the various situations I knew him to have been in during his life and backed my fancy. It was like entering a creative delirium. Pictures appeared before me which I wrote down in scenes. If I do the same thing in ten years' time, I may come up with a different story but I doubt that will happen. I doubt the energy that accompanied the writing of this treatment will ever return.

It was Tom Thompson's idea to publish my movie treatment of the Tom Wills story as a book along with photographs, sketches and paintings from that time with which to feed the reader's imaginings. And so, in this way and for these reasons, The Tom Wills Picture Show was created....

Martin Flanagan

Melbourne

THE
TOM WILLS
PICTURE
SHOW

1

1840, Western Victoria. A wagon labours across a grass plain and up a slope, surrounded by several hundred sheep and a number of shepherds. The camera lingers on the face of one of these, a rough-looking man called Miller. In the wagon is a pregnant woman of 24, a four-year-old boy and a short exuberant man of 30. This is the family of Horatio Wills. His Irish-born wife Elizabeth is clearly weary from the arduous journey overland from New South Wales. She holds her belly, there is discomfort in her face. The boy's name is Tom. They are in western Victoria only that name has not been invented. They are in the colony of Port Phillip and they are this particular area's first white settlers. He is a man who dreams grand dreams and has the drive and energy to make them real. He is the son of Edward Wills, a convict trans-ported to Botany Bay for highway robbery. He would have been hanged but for the intervention, on his behalf, of the Duke of Marlborough, thus leading to the belief that Edward Wills was an illegitimate member of the Duke of Marlborough's clan, the Churchills.

Horatio springs from the wagon. Before him are the range of rocky outcrops the Scottish   settlers who follow will call the Grampians. The local Aboriginal people, the Tjapwurrung, call the mountains Gariwerd and say it is the place where fire first fell to earth. The Wills family are surrounded by rolling hills and native grass plains. Horatio takes Tom from the cart. Holding him in his arms, he says gleefully, "Look, Tom, look! This is the new world and it is ours, ours to fashion and shape". Horatio hardly seems to notice the boy does not respond. Horatio turns to his wife. "Elizabeth," he cries. "Elizabeth, I am naming this place Ararat because here, as in the Bible, we rested". Her response is remark-ably like her son's. She merely wants to lie down. Horatio's zeal, his excite-ment, remain undiluted.

2

Six months later. A tent now stands where the wagon stopped. Elizabeth emerges, a basket with clothing in her hands, no longer pregnant. From within the tent a baby can be heard crying. She is a pale, nervous woman. We see a sudden look of fear on her face. The camera shows us what she has seen – a group of blacks camped round a waterhole several hundred metres down the slope to the west. Then she looks around, crying out, "Tom! Tom!" Dropping the basket, she cries out, "Horatio! Horatio!", and runs away towards a group of men cutting redgums 100 metres away. "The blacks are here. The blacks are here and I can't find Tom". For the first time we see fear in Horatio's face. He rushes to the tent, looks down, sees the blacks camp which has appeared in the night. To one side a group of four or five kids are playing a ball game with a stuffed possum skin. One of the kids is white. It's Tom.

"Get the guns," says Elizabeth.

"No, no, no," says Horatio, putting a calming hand across his wife's front. "No, no, leave this to me. I've dealt with native folk before. I lived among them when I was a whaler".

Horatio strides down the slope and into the blacks' camp sporting a big smile. He walks among them nodding and smiling, showing obsequious respect. Stopping in front of an old woman, he leans forward and puts on a performance, gesturing elaborately. "You – me – the same. Me – worship – the Sun". He point upwards to the sky and makes a bowing motion which then becomes a little dance. "At night – big black – me worship the moon". The old woman's impassive face at first looks puzzled. Then a woman to her left cackles at the sheer stupidity of Horatio's dance and the old woman laughs, too. Encouraged, Horatio continues, "Me jump-up whitefeller like William Buckley" He holds up his white skin. "Me blackfeller underneath". Judging Horatio to be mad but

The game of Marngrook, as played by the Latjilatji Aboriginals in Victoria; from William Blandowski's expeditions, published 1857.

harmless, the tension dissipates. Horatio believes he has persuaded the blacks he is one of them. He turns and firmly takes his small son's arm.

"Tom, we are going," he says.

The kid resists. "But I don't want to."

Horatio pulls Tom away, nodding and smiling to the Aboriginal people he passes.

3

Three years later. A ball game. Aboriginal kids plus Tom. The game is endless – it's about getting the ball, evading capture and disposing of the ball skilfully and cleverly when required to do so. There are no goals. Goals are a European idea. This game is about endless, joyful motion. Horatio appears from the side. He has no fear for Tom's safety. That is not his concern. His concern is Tom's education.

Tom, he says, Tom. Come home for your lessons. The white boy leaves but in leaving he speaks to his Tjapwurrung playmates. He speaks to them in Tjapwurrung. They reply. They have an exchange, then Tom turns and leaves, walking beside his father.

What did he say to you? asks Horatio

He asked me to come back and play. I said to him, I will, I like your games.

Horatio keeps walking.

Your lessons with me are going to be daily, Tom. A man has no chance in this world without an education.

Tom, being pulled along by his father, looks back at the camp of the blacks. Horatio, somewhat surprised to learn that he is not the centre of his son's attention, looks at what he is looking at – the camp of the blacks.

4

An Aboriginal woman, last in a line of Aboriginal women, is walking through a forest. You are hearing women's laughter and chatter when a face appears from a tree, grabs the woman, clamping a hand across her face and pulling her to the ground. It is Miller, Horatio's stockman. The next shot is of two sets of eyes – Miller's are mad and staring, imposing his will to silence on the woman. Her eyes are terrified. He holds her there until the sound of the women's laughter and chatter is some way distant. Then he rapes her.

5

Elizabeth Wills in her tent. Turns and sees black man with cold hate in his eyes. He pushes her to the ground but before he falls upon her she screams. As the sound continues, we see the scene from a different perspective – from outside the tent. We see Horatio and the men working, erecting a shed for storage. Hearing the scream Horatio runs for the tent, shouting, Elizabeth! Elizabeth. One of the men with Horatio -not Miller - picks up a gun and fires into the air. He does it in several directions so the noise gets out as far as possible while Horatio and Miller run for the tent. Inside the tent, Elizabeth Wills' face is one of manic desperation as she holds off this black man who has one hand pressing on her face. Distracted by the gunshots, the black man looks up; in that instant, she hits him with a candle stick. The sound of running can be heard approaching the tent, the sound of voices. The black man pushes off her – it can be seen he has not succeeded in raping her – her dress is not pulled up – and runs off. Horatio Wills, pulling open the tent door is met with a distraught wife and her long shuddering cry. He embraces her, comforting her.

6

It's night time in the bush. The shooting party is out, Horatio Wills among them. They creep through the bush, guns in hand. A man up ahead signals them to stop and points. Through the trees can be seen a fire, a camp - Aboriginal men, women and children. The leader waves his hand to indicate the whites should spread out. Horatio goes to the right with another man. The other man stops Horatio and points, directing his attention to an Aboriginal woman sitting on a log. She is naked from the waist up. She has an infant feeding from her right breast. The man makes a gesture to ensure Horatio knows which Aboriginal person he is referring to – the woman with the infant. Then he takes up his rifle, takes aim and fires. The woman is flung about by the impact of the bullet, the baby drops to the ground. The man turns to Horatio with a clenched fist salute and a huge grin on his face. He's enjoyed shooting a woman with a baby at her breast like he's enjoyed shooting a duck on the first day of the duck shooting season. Horatio is incredulous. By now, others have started firing, Aboriginal people are falling over, others are screaming and, in panic, running everywhere. Horatio hasn't moved, hasn't lifted his gun. His shocked eyes are on the man beside him. When he turns it is to see carnage and the Aboriginal mother writhing on the ground.

7

"God, God, God". A tormented Horatio Wills is marching up and down a paddock, arms clasped behind his back, Bible in his hands. "Only you who know everything understands". He looks towards the Grampians/ Gariwerd, magnificent and blue and strange to him. He looks towards the blacks camp. They've all gone. "Only you know, Lord!" shouts Horatio to the heavens. "Only you know!" He looks back towards the house and sees a boy, Tom, running towards him.

"Are they back?" cries Tom in an excited voice. "Are the blacks back?"

(Top) Aboriginal mother and child, (lower); Mounted Police attack Blacks, by Godfrey Muundey 1852.

"No," says Horatio. "No, they've gone away".

Tom is disappointed. "I have no-one to play with".

Horatio is touched, wants to help. "Next week I'll pack up the dray and we'll go over to the McGoverns. You can play with William".

"William's games are boring. The blacks' game are fun".

Horatio looks back, knowing and troubled, at the empty space that was the camp of the blacks.

8

Horatio and Elizabeth are sitting for tea along with their three-year-old daughter. They are in a wattle hut Horatio has erected while building a colonial mansion red brick mansion on the site where the original tent was. Horatio says, "We'll wait for Tom". The family waits. Horatio, very much the head of the house, is waiting for Tom's arrival to say grace.

When did you last see Tom? he asks

Elizabeth: Two hours ago. Then, she adds in a low voice, knowing it will make trouble, He missed his afternoon lessons.

Suddenly, a back door crashes open, Tom comes running in, obviously excited.

"The blacks are back!," he cries, his voice full of joy.

"What - ?!" cries a startled Horatio – this is his nightmare. He pushes away from the table, runs out of the house. In the half-light of evening, down near the water pool he sees a fire and some black figures moving about, although not so many as before. Horatio looks down and sees Tom who has run with him.

I spent all afternoon playing with them, says Tom.

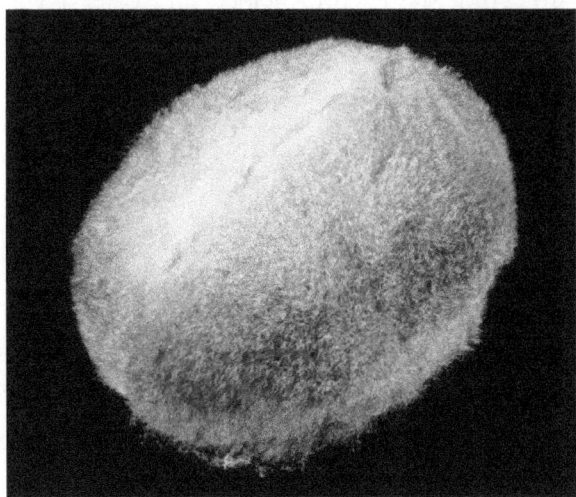

(Top) Horatio Wills 1859, (lower); A possum fur football as used by Aboriginals in the game known as Marngrook.

Horatio stops what he is doing, kneels down on one leg, grabs Tom's shoulders and says: Say that to me again, boy. What did you do with the blacks this afternoon?

Tom, puzzled by Horatio's great seriousness, I said I played with them.

You played with the blacks!

Yes, father.

Horatio's trickiness comes to the fore. Taking his son by the hand, he walks with him down into the camp of the blacks, entering it with extravagant bows and grins. Stopping in front of the same old woman, he says, This white picanniny same as black picanniny. The old woman nods. Horatio puts on a big grin. "Me same as you. Me worship sun and moon," he says, and begins his dance. He walks back to the house, as ever pulling along Tom, whose eyes are back on the camp. Entering the house, he is met by a very anxious wife.

"I have won them over," declares Horatio, running his hand through the boy's hair. "And Master Tom helped me. Later I will take them some supplies".

His wife looks sick with fear.

"But then they will stay"

Horatio: They have nowhere else to go. They will be shot.

Elizabeth (rising): This half-world of white and black is Hell!

She goes to the hut's other room, which is in part the kitchen, and with Horatio not looking, opens a cupboard takes out a bottle of brandy, pours a small glss and has a swig, then quickly puts it away and stands, eyes closed, breast heaving.

9

1845. Elizabeth approaches Horatio. Her tone is concerned but not fearful – she's dealt with this situation before.

Tom's gone missing again, she says. He's gone with the blacks.

Horatio looks down the valley to the blacks' empty camp-site and to the forest beyond.

Don't worry about him – he'll be back. He knows the bush as well as they do.

10

A corroboree. A game of Aboriginal football being played. The dominant feature of the game is kicking a stuffed possum skin high in the air and leaping to catch it. If it were possible to involve for Melbourne player Liam Jurrah (an initiated Warlpiri man), we could get him to take a high mark in this fashion….

11

A few hours later. Horatio and Elizabeth sit ostentatiously waiting to eat with daughter and second son. Crashing of a door, Tom runs in – sees that he is late.

Where have you been, Tom?

Tom, sensing the seriousness of the situation, With the blacks, Father.

Horatio: I thank you for being honest, Tom. Had you not been so I would have punished you. What did you do with the blacks?

I saw the game played by the men. They fly like birds. It's the best game –

His eyes are alight and Horatio can see it.

Did you play?

Yes. Tom's looking away but he still can't deny his excitement. Yes, yes, I played. I'm a white cockatoo. This is Grugidj country, Father. White cockatoo country.

Well, you'll be leaving it soon, Tom. I'm sending you to a boarding school in Melbourne and, from there, to a school in England – the best school in England.

He says it in a way he hopes will make the school sound exciting for Tom. Tom nods with the flicker of a polite smile on his face but then he looks way and returns to his memories of what he's seen that day. Now that was exciting, he didn't have to try and pretend like he did with his Father who drove him like a man drives a car.

I don't want to leave here, Father. I will try harder at my lessons.

You're not growing up out here one more day than I can help it, says Elizabeth shortly.

To which Horatio adds: I mean to make a man of you, Tom.

12

1850. Rugby school dormitory. Tom's 15. He's on the verge of manhood & strongly built. He has the rhythmic walk of someone who's good at sport, who's got power in his hips and arms and legs and the confidence that goes with all of that. He's being shown his study – a small, narrow room with a bed, a desk, a chair - by an old porter who puts down a heavy suitcase of Tom's on a bed.

Thanks, mate, Tom. He slaps a half crown in the old man's hand. He has an Australian manner. This is important because, by the time he returns to Australia in six years' time, his manner will be English. The old porter is taken with Tommy's generosity.

Young sir?

Yes, says Tom, turning.

The young gentlemen might seek to have a little fun with you tonight, if you know what I mean. It's called ragging.

Tom: Do you mean – they want to play games.

Yes, sir. Games you may not like.

Tom stops and looks at the porter.

We'll see about that, he says.

13

A gang of boys some as old as 18. There is a wild, grinning excitement about them. They stop outside the door to Tom's room, hold fingers to lips, open the door, charge – and almost as immediately stop. Those outside the door pull back. An Aboriginal war-cry is heard whereupon a spear passes through their midst and buries its quivering self in the wall opposite. The boys re-emerge, fear in their eyes. They run away, feet clattering in the hall way. Tom appears, naked from the waist up in the attitude of a warrior. He is painted up, killing boomerang in one hand, nulla nulla in the other.

14

Next day. Tom, in Rugby school uniform, warily approaches the cricket nets. He is the talk of the school, the other boys watch him from a distance, whispering his name as he passes. That's the Australian who threw the spear, says a voice. He reaches the net. A batsman is facing two bowlers. Tom stands and watches, picking up a ball. A break in the bowling appears, he runs in and bowls underarm. It is an action like bowling in a ten-pin bowling alley. He is good at it. The ball skids towards the batsman who is obliged to block it back down the pitch.

One of the Rugby bowlers. "We don't bowl under-arm at Rugby any more. We bowl round-arm. It creates much more speed. Watch Maurice."

Maurice, the other Rugby bowler, runs in. His action must be authentic but no more than moderately impressive by contrast with what follows. The next shot is the first of many in which the actor playing Tom must have sporting ability or the ability to convey sporting ability. Tom's run-in is immediately strong, potent, rhythmic. He delivers the ball round-arm (like Sri Lankan slinger Lasith Malinga). The ball is through the batsman, his stumps are clattered.

We see the face of the boy who told Tom to bowl round-arm. He's impressed.

So you're a bowler, Wills.

Wills looks at the boys around him, none of whom he trusts, but conscious also that he is being given an identity that might allow him to pass through this strange new world.

Yes, he says. I'm a bowler.

15

Victorian Legislative Assembly 1855. Horatio Wills is trying to speak to a debate on penal reform. On the other side of the house a member is shouting, "You'd know about being a convict, Horatio – your old man was one!" The man's supporters laugh loudly in support of what he has said. One, a young lawyer, jumps to his feet and cries, "The convict stain has no place in the free colony of Victoria". The voices against Horatio grow more rowdy, more numerous. Horatio stops. He despises what he sees building against him. Finally, in desperation, he cries, "You may not listen to me, but one day you will listen to my son – my son who is at Rugby is going to be a great leader!"

More laughter.

16

The Rugby playing field. Tom is captaining a rugby team. It's the first time we see him as an adult. He is talking quietly, compellingly, to his players. He talks quietly because he doesn't have to shout. He's got the game worked out. "Our front line will be the Heavy Brigade - the big boys in height and brawn. Behind them, the Light Brigade – the runners, the dodgers, the fliers".

All 60 boys in Wills' house are in the team from the tallest to the shortest, from the oldest to the youngest.

Wills to the big boys. "Push and hold your ground over the ball. I will burrow it back to you – ". He points to a lean fair-headed boy who looks like he can run. "Young-uns stay behind. We'll bring you into the game when we can provide you with protection". Camera lands on an even younger boy, six or seven. We'll call him Green. Green is eager to play.

The two teams rush and meet like screaming armies. A rolling maul begins. Green runs to the side and leaps on to the pack. He is knocked down by a big boy from the other house with a deliberate blow – a backward sweep of his arm that catches the small boy in the face. Green goes down with a cry.

Wills is with him in a flash, comforting him, dabbing at his bloodied mouth with a handkerchief.

Who did it?, he says.

Williams, says the boy holding his face, pointing. Green has blood around his mouth and is clearly hurt.

Wills re-enters the fray. We see him work his way towards Williams. The next moment the mass scrum rolls away and Williams is seen on the ground, looking surprised and holding his broken nose.

Camera returns to Green whose eyes shine with pride and pleasure. "Wills is the best captain!" he says.

17

1855. An English cricket match. Tommy and Lord Harry, dressed in the elaborate costume of the I Zingari cricket club, lounge in easy chairs on the verandah of the pavilion. A crowd of several hundred watches.

Lord Harry has a cigarette holder and is smoking. He's a gentleman of pleasure, cricket is one of his pleasures but he has plenty of others. He admires Wills in the way that an art collector admires a great painting, in the way that a racehorse owner admires a champion thoroughbred. He knows Wills is a great talent at that most exciting moment in his career – when he is first revealing the full dimensions of that talent to the public.

You have given us a chance, Wills, even if you did it by occasionally bowling high.

Cricket is a man's game, Harry (we notice that Tom now speaks like an English gentleman). The batsman runs the risk of being hit with a hard ball if he misses. If the ball is short enough, he runs the risk of being hit in the head. That's how it should be, Harry. Wills looks him in the eye. Tells you who really wants to play, who really wants to be out there, in the line of fire, who's good enough to stand his ground against the very best opponent. That's what sport's about Harry. Real sport, sport worth playing, not children's stuff.

Lord Harry: Do you think about anything other than sport, Tom?

THE CUT.

Tom – he puts on a devilish grin –I think about the parties at the end of each day's play. That's why I play with you, Harry. You have good parties.

This statement, like much of what Tom says, can be read two ways. It may mean he has no respect for Lord Harry and his type. He continues smiling at Lord Harry, nods and takes his leave. We watch him walk away – his strong, rhythmic walk, his confident air. He watches the play as he walks. Out there, on the playing field, he's as good as any man in England. There are older players who still have his measure in part but that part gets less each time the play. A group comes towards him – a young gentleman with two young women, maybe a brother and two sisters. After they pass Tom, the young man says, "That's young Mr Wills from Rugby. The papers say he is one of the best young cricketers in England. He plays for Kent. He has already been invited to play in a touring All-England XI."

The girls' eyes follow Tom, this magnificent young man like a magnificent young stallion. Turning and noticing their attention, he gives them a knowing wink.

18

Horatio is talking to himself, writing a letter to Tom, in his colonial mansion. The camera goes from seeing Horatio inside his study to seeing him from outside outside his study. The land is in large part colonised. The bush is beaten back. It is a vista of hills and paddocks with the Grampians/Gariwerd in the background. We hear Horatio's rising voice –

"By now you should be fluent in French and you can hardly write in English! From what I can see, your life is spent in playing games! Games are for children, Thomas, and you are going to become a man. I am calling you home. I have found you a job in a solicitor's office in Collingwood…."

19

Melbourne Cricket Ground 1856. Inside the change room in the members' pavilion. First we see a foot. A brocaded shoe. Then we see impeccably pressed white trousers, a colourful belt. A formal white shirt over which is pulled the coat of the I Zingari club. The I Zingari club colours are yellow, red and black. From darkness, through the fire, into the light. I Zingari cricketers are a knightly code who play cricket by day and party by night. Tom has played and partied with them for the past year as well as representing Cambridge University, although he only stayed in the University for the week of the game. He has also played in Dublin for the first All-Irish team. Tom Wills will play with anyone but this day he is out to make a particularly strong impression. He completes his costume with a pasha's brocaded cap. The other men are all dressed in conservative fashion – white shirts, white trousers, belts. They look amateurs by comparison and you sense already their resentment of Tom.

Outside the change rooms are the mob – the ugly street creatures of Melbourne that haunt the imagination of the Melbourne middle class. They are not called the fans. They are called the mob, the same word used during the revolution in Paris and all the revolts in the 50 years since. Tommy steps out in the costume of the I Zingari club, looks straight at the mob who start cat-calling, nods and grins. He walks across to the loudest (I hope he will be played by Joffa, the king of the Collingwood cheer squad), puts out his hand and says, Tom Wills.

Fred Morgan, says the man, taken aback. The other gentlemen sportsmen of the colony insist on being called "Mister".

"Fred," says Tom, taking a coin from his hand and slipping it into Fred's, "Fred, this afternoon when I take a wicket – and I'll take plenty - I want you to enter the spirit of the game. I want you to shout out and make plenty of noise. I'll meet you and your mates afterwards and buy you all a drink".

Victoria's cricketers, 1858, (left to right): Gideon Elliott, Barton Grindrod, George Marshall, James Bryant and Tom Wills.

Gee, thanks, says Morgan, also taken aback, Thanks Mr Wills.

Tommy's a yard or so from him.

Call me Tommy, he says with a grin, giving the thumbs up signal – the one used by working class colonial males to acknowledge one other - as he does. He then trots out into the middle of the arena. Fred leans over the fence and shouts, "GO TOOOOMMMMYYYY!"

20

Seven hours later. Inside the Melbourne Cricket Club change rooms.

End of the day, a group of sweaty defeated men.

One of them says, Wills destroyed us.

Another: He's already got the mob on side.

Another: At least he'll be on our side when we play New South Wales.

A character we will come to recognise as William Tennant: Wills is on no-one's side but his own.

The door opens. In comes Wills, the spirit of optimism.

That wasn't too bad, lads. I believe we can beat New South Wales.

We've never beaten New South Wales.

There's always a first time for everything, believe you me. We just have to make one change to the team.

What's that?

I have to be made captain.

Camera goes to the face of Tennant. By his shock and displeasure, we sense he may have been the captain up until this moment.

(Top) Tom Wills 1858; (lower) Inter-Colonial Match, Victoria v New South Wales, held at the Melbourne Cricket Ground, January 1858.

21

Top end of Bourke Street, Melbourne. Lots of people about, including theatre-goers. The victorious Victorian XI are out celebrating their win over New South Wales. Passing a theatre, one of the team stops and speaks to a group of young working class women standing outside a theatre. The camera stops and for the first time we see Sally. She's Irish, red-haired, pale-skinned, brave and spirited.

Young buck full of drunken confidence: Ladies, don't waste your hard-won pennies on a second-rate show. Come and celebrate a first-class victory. We are the Victorian XI. Today, for the first time, we defeated New South Wales. This man – he reaches out and grabs Wills who is passing in a head-lock, kissing him on the cheek – is our beloved captain, Mr TW Wills.

Wills laughingly untangles himself from his team-mate's arm. He's very drunk. Come on ladies, he says. Let's have some fun. The night is young and I intend to dance to dawn.

You can dance, can you? Says Sally challengingly.

Oh yes, says Wills, his eyes focussing upon her. I do the dingo dance of western Victoria.

The dingo dance? She says. That's be something to see.

Immediately, he drops into an Aboriginal dance honouring the dingo, we see its stealth, its private intelligence, its public face closed to scrutiny.

She applauds.

Young buck: Wills, come on. I didn't say you had to talk to them. I was just trying to pick up some tarts that we could fuck later on.

Sally, indignant, to Tom: He called my friends and I tarts. What are you going to do about it?

Wills looks at her, taking in what she has said. Then he turns and looks at the young buck, swaying slightly as he does. He looks back at Sally and in that instant, when the young buck thinks he is looking away, rushes him, grabbing him by the collar, folding him in half and running him face first into a horse trough, ducking him once, twice, three times, shouting, "Wash your mouth out with water!!!"

Sally and her friends are delighted. Wills releases the young buck who stands, water pouring down his face, slime in his ears.

You're mad, Wills, he hisses, as he runs off. There is fear and disgust in his eyes. You're fucking mad!

He is of no consequence to Wills who is looking at Sally. Bowing, he says, And now you can dance for me.

She looks at him, smiles and says, Not here.

22

An hour later. Tom sits beneath a gas lamp on the edge of Melbourne parkland. It is quiet and peaceful. On the opposite side of the circle of light cast by the lamp stands Sally. He is watching her intently, an excited grin on his lips. One of her feet protrudes and is pointed downwards to the earth, her dress is raised and she performs for him a traditional Irish dance with great dignity. It is a dance of physical precision and velocity performed with an impassive face and the straightest of backs. The dancer doesn't invite the attention – the dance does. Tom's taken with her.

23

Next morning. Tom's hotel room. They have something in common – at minimum, a silence they can share. You can see from his face he has something on his mind. She lies across his chest. Her voice is beautifully low.

Sally: So, who's the great Tom Wills when he's home?

Tom (faintly irritated, getting up out of bed. He's naked): Don't ask questions about me.

Why not?

Because there are no answers to them. I'm not like anyone I know. I never have been. I've given up trying to know me. I just do things. . I play games. I'm Tom Wills. Right now I'm famous . Everyone thinks I'm wonderful except my father.

He starts shuffling through his wardrobe for clothes, sloppily pulling on trousers. He's still half-drunk.

Sally: Why do you talk like a toff?

Tom (turning) Do I? Well, a gentleman in England told me it was very important to sound like a gentleman, even if you weren't one. He said it's amazing what you'll get away with and it does seem to be the way...

He pulls a pocket watch out of his coat.

Oh, Jesus, he says. It's half past nine. I'm late for work again.

He pulls on the remainder of his clothes then throws the room key to Sally. As he's going out the door, he says, "Lock up when you leave and leave the key under the mat".

We're left looking at Sally sitting up in bed. She's smiling.

24

Committee Room of the Melbourne Cricket Club. Present are two characters who will prove central to the narrative – William Tennant, the man Wills displaced as captain of the Victorian XI, and JB Ellis. Both Tennant and Ellis are Cambridge men. They are also journalists. The Melbourne Cricket Club is an offshoot of the Melbourne Club which runs the colony in conjunction with the Legislative Council and the Argus newspaper for whom Ellis writes.

Right, gentlemen, says the president, the matter of Wills. Do we offer him the position of secretary of the Melbourne Cricket Club?

Well, says Ellis, he is the premier player in the colony and we aspire to be the premier club.

Tennant: He'll take the place over. He has no regard for anyone's opinion but his own.

Ellis: Tennant, he just captained Victoria to its first ever victory over New South Wales. I hardly need tell you what a boon that has been for cricket in the colony and, indeed, the colony. He's the hero of the hour. If we don't get him, one of the other clubs will. We risk losing our public prestige.

Tennant pulls back, shaking his head, but says nothing.

President: We are agreed then. We will offer Mr Wills the position of secretary of the Melbourne Cricket Club.

25

Same room, a few days later. "The first thing we have to do" – the camera leaves Wills's face, he is addressing the MCC committee – "is start a football competition".

The committee looks startled.

President: We are a cricket club, Mr Wills.

Wills in a sunny, pleasant, re-assuring way, Yes, but we are the leading club in the colony, Mr President, and we must continue to lead. I want to defeat New South Wales in Sydney. I need a football competition to keep my cricketers fit in winter.

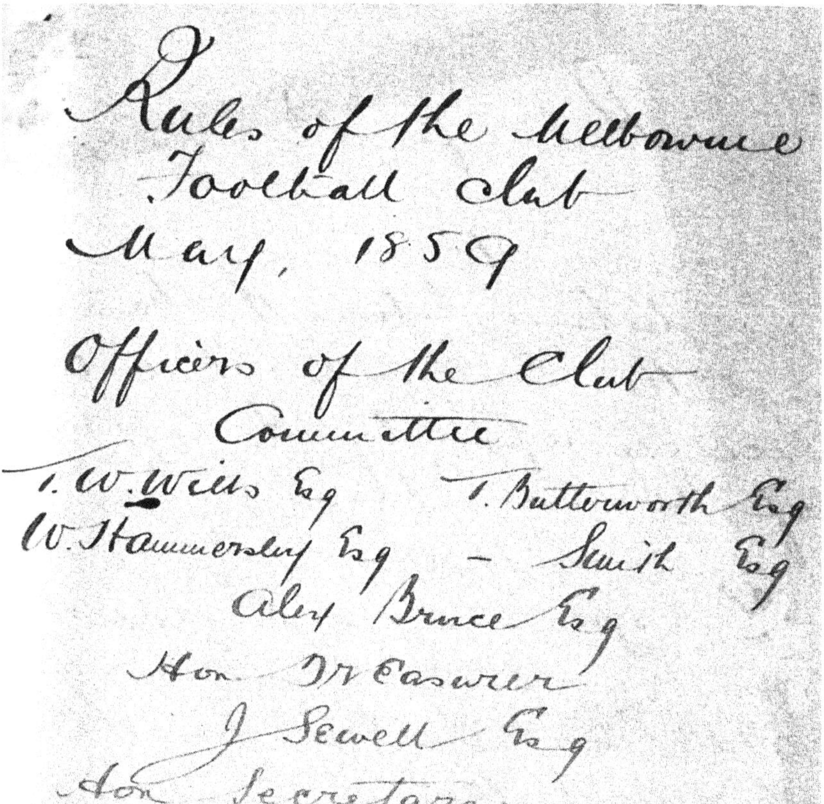

Rules of the Melbourne
Football Club
May, 1859

Officers of the Club
Committee

T. W. Wills Esq   T. Butterworth Esq

W. Hammersley Esq   — Smith Esq

Alex Bruce Esq

Hon Treasurer

J Sewell Esq

Hon Secretary

J B Thompson Esq

Tennant: And what code of football are you proposing, Wills? Every school in England has its own rules.

A game of our own. That's what I'm proposing - a game of our own!

He accompanies his words with a big bright grin. The committeemen are profoundly uncertain.

Oh, and by the way, gentlemen, I have accepted an invitation to captain the Melbourne Grammar School in their first ever game of football against Scotch College next week. Dr Bromley, the headmaster of the Grammar school, was much impressed by "Tom Brown's Schooldays". Tom Brown, as you no doubt know, preceded me as captain of the Rugby First XI. His real name was Hughes.

He has the committee eating out of his hand.

The president: Well, that sounds good to me. The other committeemen murmur.

Oh, and one other thing, says Wills, getting up. I have undertaken to play cricket this Saturday for Collingwood.

Collingwood -?! Says a committeeman. They're a slum team.

That's right, that's why we're going to support them .

Across the table, William Tennant, the man Wills replaced as captain of the Victorian XI, can be seen shaking his head: Wills, this may sound childishly simple – but we hired you to play for us.

No, says Wills, holding up a finger in the manner of an orator. You hired me to maintain the position of the Melbourne Cricket Club as the pre-eminent cricket club in the colony. And that will require change, constant change.

Wills has won the day – just. He won't win many more.

26

Football match. The two captains are discussing the rules for the day's play, surrounded by the other players who basically look like solicitors having a day out. They are all of a certain class to which Wills has access through (1) being a Rugby man and (2) being the best sportsman in the colony and (3) being the secretary of the Melbourne Cricket Club. Wills is shaking his head and saying, No off-side rule.

Other captain: No off-side rule? All the school games in England have off-side rules.

Wills: The off-side rule is for captains who cannot set a field for players ahead of the ball. It's half a game. This way brings the full field into play.

In a tree above them, a noisy pack of white cockatoos rise up squawking.

See, he says with a grin on his face. They agree with me.

No-one quite knows what to say – Wills is the dominant character in the local sporting scene. He continues on:

And one other change of rule. As captain of the home side, I get to choose the ball. (He opens a bag and takes out an oval-shaped ball). Here it is.

The others are surprised.

Other captain: We always play with a round ball.

Wills: Get your best man to kick the round ball as far as he can in the air and I will kick this twice as far. (He holds up the oval-shaped ball like it is an object of wonder). This ball was displayed in the Great Exhibition in London. It is used at the Rugby school. It makes for a faster, more open game.

JB Ellis: Oh, come on, Wills. What's next? Octagonal cricket balls?!

Wills: I insist on my right as home captain to select the ball for the day.

The rest trudge off suspiciously. We see the game begin. The other players can't handle the oval ball. When they try and kick it on the run, the ball squirts sideways. We see Wills effortlessly gather the ball and then, with earnest intensity, punt it downfield (he could punt the ball 55 yards).

Ellis, unimpressed, is watching from the side with William Tennant.

Tennant: Have you ever noticed how every rule Wills introduces works to his advantage? It's the same in cricket he wants to bowl high. He consistently bowled high when he played for Collingwood against the Melbourne Club. Some of the chaps told me they were in fear of their life. One of them called him a cheat and Wills struck him.

Ellis: Do you read The Argus? I mean to write something about him in Monday's edition. No names of course but everyone will know who I'm talking about.

27

Tom and Sally in bed. Room semi-dark. Loud, insistent knocking on the door. Sally rises, knowing this is unusual and shakes Tom awake.

Horatio (through the door): Tom! It's your father!

Tom startled into consciousness. Whispers to Sally, "Quick, under the bed".

Coming father, he calls, reaching for clothes, pulling open the curtains. Reaching the door and opening it, he says sweetly, "I would've ordered breakfast if I'd known you were coming".

He is met by a quietly furious Horatio holding a copy of the Argus which he brandishes in Tom's face.

Horatio: "You struck a member of the Melbourne Club. You know the grief people associated with that club have given me. They are the ones who hissed Son of a Convict! Son of a Convict! every time I stood to speak in the parliament. You have empowered my enemies. Tom (weakly) Father…he called me a cheat…..no gentleman in England would allow that to pass.

Horatio: You have gambling debts all over Melbourne. You won't work and the only thing that interests you is games. I sent you to Rugby to make a man of boy and they have sent me back – a boy with a man's conviction as to his childish purposes! But I grant you this much, Thomas - you have given me new resolution. I can go no further in this society - I am returning to the frontier. That is where a man can really make something of himself. And you, my son, are coming with me. If you do not, I will disinherit you.

Horatio means it, and Tom knows it. He slumps into a chair, throws back his head, puts his hands to his forehead.

Horatio: The new frontier is Queensland and that is where we're going.

Horatio speaking with quiet intensity, knowing also that Sally is somewhere in the room & listening: And as for you picking up that slut off the streets and installing her in this hotel at my expense, you should know that you have visited a scalding shame upon your mother.

Horatio leaves, slamming shut the door behind him. Sally emerges from behind the curtains. It's the first time she's seen Tom defeated.

Sally: What are you going to do?

Tom: What choice do I have?

She dresses, then, turning to go, says, "Tom, you ducked a young man in a horse trough for calling me a tart. When your father called me a slut, you said nothing".

Tom says nothing. Sally, noting his silence, leaves.

28

Central Queensland 1861. A massive flock of thousands of sheep. A party of about 20. A wagon with the Bakers, a father, mother, three boys – including 15-year-old James - and a baby. A wagon pulled by oxen with supplies and a giant wool press. A couple of young men Tom's age plus older ones of Horatio's vintage, including Miller. Horatio, face ecstatic, strides alongside Tom, puts an arm around him, embracing him vigorously.

This is God's country, Tom!! This is our country!! Are you not glad you made the trip?

Yes, Father, I am glad.

He doesn't match Horatio's enthusiasm but says it good-naturedly. In fact, he's missing out on the opportunity to play against the First All-England XI to tour Australia in a match that will attract one in eight of Melbourne's population to the MCG.

Two horsemen approach thunderously. The leader is a young man in his 20s, dark-haired, English. He has a pistol in a holster on his hip, a carbine under his leg. He jumps from his horse, hand extended to Horatio.

I am your neighbour, Jesse Grierson. I have come to warn you – you will need to carry arms. The blacks in this part of the country are trouble. I had to shoot two of them the other day for stealing sheep.

Horatio is watching Grierson with a closed expression.

How long have you been in the colonies, Mr Grierson?

Eighteen months.

Well, I've been here all my life and I've been handling the blacks since before you were a boy. I intend to placate them and win them to my purpose so, no, I will not be wearing firearms and nor will anyone in my party. There will be no shooting of blacks on my land and I'll thank you to remember it.

Grierson's face crosses with a frown. Realising Horatio is serious, he bounds back upon his horse, shaking his head. You have been warned, Mr Wills, he says.

With his companion, rides off as thunderously as he came. Horatio turns back to Tom, as cheerful as before.

See that line of green over there, Tom. If there's water in the creek, we'll be making it our base camp.

Tom looks at the row of trees, then turns and looks after Grierson. We see his fear, his uncertainty.

29

Next morning. We see Tom awake, lift his head and quickly take in that they are surrounded by blacks. They are not a war party but they do have some weapons, boomerangs, spears, nulla nullas. There are men, women, children. They are viewing the white party – among the first whites they have ever seen - with unspoken suspicion. Tom doesn't panic – he is equal to the situation. His father is asleep beside him on the ground. He rouses him with calm urgency.

Father, he says, shaking him slightly, you need to wake. We have visitors.

Horatio wakes, startled, but quickly regains his self-possession.

Ah my friends, he says grandly, getting to his feet. We were hoping to meet you soon. He raises a finger, keeping one eye on them all the time. I have something for you.

The party's equipment has been unloaded. There are boxes, pots, pans. Horatio goes to a particular box, opens it and takes out lengths of cloth, colourful handkerchiefs, mirrors, bags of boiled sweets. He turns and approaches the blacks, carrying the goods in his arms.

Stopping in front of one of the old women, he says, You, me, the same. Pointing upwards, he says, Me worship the sun.

He starts his dance. The blacks view him coldly. Sensing his father is on the wrong track, Tom steps forward and says something in Tjapwurrung, What is the name of your people?

They have some sense he is speaking an Aboriginal language but don't know what he says - they don't reply but they watch him with more interest than they watch his father.

Horatio puts his load on the ground in front of the blacks. Taking one of the handkerchiefs, he approaches a woman but she moves away. From his pocket, Horatio takes out a boiled lolly wrapped in paper. Approaching a child, he elaborately unwraps the lolly and puts it in his mouth, making much of the joy it gives him. "Yum, yum". He approaches a child but the child shies away from him.

There is a moment of stand-off. Then one of the older Aboriginal men steps forward and, having picked up everything Horatio has put down, returns to his group. He speaks in language and the group moves away but there is no warmth from them. The blacks move away.

Horatio is well pleased with his efforts. Well, well, he says. That was the first step. They have accepted our gifts. Happy relations are on the way.

Tom (urgently): Father, they are not friendly – you must tell the men to carry arms.

Horatio: I will do nothing of the kind.

Tom: Father, there will be payback for the two blacks Grierson shot. If they think Grierson is one of us, we will be attacked.

Native Sepulchre, by ST Gill, 1864.

Horatio fatally misunderstands the nature of Tom's concern, patting him on the arm and giving him a big grin.

Not losing your nerve, are you Tom? I always thought you were a brave young man.

30

Night. Inside Horatio's tent. He tosses around in a restless sleep, begins murmuring, talking to himself. He is mumbling in a hurried way, "You alone know, God,….you alone know". In his dream we are on the punitive raid Horatio went on twenty years before in western Victoria. We see it all – silently – the leader instructing them to fan out, the glee of the man who shot the woman in the breast, the woman on the ground, bleeding from the breast, her fallen baby. Now, as Horatio watches, she rises from death and seems to walk towards him.

He wakes up, not screaming as in a wild cry, but with his senses prised wildly open. A hideous possibility has just entered his consciousness. He doesn't know what it means. What he knows is that this is not his land. Maybe it can become so by use but at this moment it is their land, they know it best. In fact, they know it intimately while he is a stranger. Horatio looks about. There is no solace from his terrible nightmare in his surroundings. We see him make his way towards where Tom lies, looking about him as he does. We see Tom lying awake, pistol in hand.

Thomas, says Horatio.

Father, whispers Tom. He sees that Horatio's behaviour is odd, out of the ordinary.

Tom, says Horatio, looking about, tomorrow I want you to take young James Baker and walk back to Rainworth station. I want you to collect the dray we left behind.

Attack on Store Dray, by ST Gill, 1864.

Tom says nothing but we see his eyes absorbing the knowledge that all is not well, gripping his pistol.

I expect you to be away three days.

Tom, rising, You cannot ask me to go now, Father! When everyone is in danger. This is when young men must fight.

Horatio: Tom, it is your Father's command.

31

Next day, Tom and a 15-year-old boy with packs on their backs. Horatio's eyes are glittering. The old sunshine is back in his smile and handshake but the eyes reveal emotion. .

All the best, old boy, he says to Tom. There is a love that is clear between them. Horatio nods to the road and says, On your way.

Tom and James head south, two people walking. After five seconds of seeing them from behind, we see them from alongside.

Tom: Did you gave that pistol I gave you to your mother?"

James: Yes, Mr Wills.

They walk on, Tom constantly scanning his surroundings.

32

Three days later. A dray being pulled by a pair of bullocks, Tom walking on one side, James Baker on the other. We see them from behind, get the pace and rhythm of their walk and follow them as they come in sight of the Wills camp and – stop! Then drop their bullwhips and run towards the pile of bodies being lowered into the mass grave. We see Baker, we see his wife, both battered around the head and bleeding and dead. So too the Baker baby, the young men of the party, Miller with a spear in his guts. All dead, everyone dead. We see three of Grierson's men lowering the bodies into the grave. We hear the sound of running feet, see a pair of hands grab one of the men doing the shovelling, saying, Where's Father? Where's Father. We hear panic in his voice. The man points to a grave some 20 metres away.

We buried your father on his own.

Tom rushes to the grave, throws himself upon it sobbing and shouting, Father, I tried to warn you!!!

The word warn sounds like it comes from the pits of Hell.

We hear the sound of thundering horses. Grierson leads in a posse of squatters he has rounded up, all armed, plus the Native Police.

We will have them by dawn, says Grierson to the man who has spoken to Tom, and we'll kill the lot.

Are you taking young Mr Wills? says the man, nodding to Tom who hasn't moved and lies weeping.

Tom: Father, I could have saved you and the others

Grierson shakes his head. He's of no use in that state.

The party ride off.

33

A night scene. All we see is carnage beneath a blue moon. We see men and women cut down by rifle fire. We see a child get its head blown off.

*(Top) The Wills Tragedy... a watercolour by TG Moyle 1861; (lower)
Horatio Will's grave near Sprinsure, Queensland.*

34

The next morning, exhausted after hours of riding and killing, the punitive party returns to the Wills camp.

Grierson: They'll not trouble you again, Mr Wills.

Tom nods. He is composed, or much moreso than when we last saw him.

Tom: I have sworn on my father's grave to make this the best station in Queensland.

Pause, Grierson doesn't respond. Then he says:

Mr Wills, what happened here is one battle in a war being fought across the length of Queensland. I take it that any blacks encountered on your station will be shot on sight.

Tom looks at Gregson: Yes, he says.

35

Geelong, 1862. Elizabeth Wills and her lawyer, Mr Pickles. He is a friend of Horatio's and a man of similar age. Elizabeth is fraught and emotional. Unbeknowns to herself or Horatio, she was pregnant when he left. The baby, a daughter, has been born but is unwell. She is 44, has nine children, no husband and is having trouble with Tom.

Pickles (rising and guiding, Elizabeth to her chair) Mrs Wills…

Elizabeth (we see how fraught she is) The last year has been a very difficult one for me, Mr Pickles. When my husband left on his great Queensland adventure, neither of us knew I was pregnant. Then he was murdered most horribly, leaving me with nine children to care for. And now my son Thomas demands we send him money so he can invest in the property. I have told him repeatedly in letters that there is no money, that his father

Mounted Police and Blacks, by Godfrey Mundy 1852.

spent everything he had on buying the property and equipping his party and now this -

She holds out a letter which has been sent to her by Pickles' law firm. Pickles face shows his genuine concern.

As you know, your husband was a dear friend of mine. It was with great regret that I informed you that Thomas has been drawing on the station funds without the approval of the executors of your husband's will.

Elizabeth is nearly a broken woman.

Pickles: Leave it with me, Mrs Wills.

36

Tom on horseback returning to the crude slab hut that serves as his home finds a stranger waiting for him. It's Pickles. Tom dismounts, walks to meet him as a Queensland property owner might. Tom is the first child and eldest son of Horatio Wills. He is the man of the family and a station owner and he walks with that pride. Pickles puts out his hand.

Mr Wills, he says. I am Bernard Pickles, a solicitor of Geelong and friend of your late father's. I am also the executor of his will.

Tom (excited). You want me to show you round! You have come to confirm my scheme of investments for the property.

No, Mr Wills, I have come to inform you that you have been replaced as manager of the property by your brother Cedric.

Tom (as if he senses a mistake) I am the first child, the eldest son. Cedric is younger than me.

Yes, Mr Wills, younger in years but older in every other way.

My mother will support me.

Victorian cricketers, 1863, with Tom Wills in striped shirt photographed by Patrick Dawson, Hamilton.

No, Mr Wills, she will not. Neither your family nor the trustees of your father's estate has confidence in you.

We see a look of shock on Tom's face, a pained awareness dawning in his head.

37

1863. The Melbourne Cricket Ground. Tom on the balcony of the Members', in whites. He is 27, in his sporting prime. He's a master of both games he plays, football and cricket. He sits alone. He's a different Tom Wills to the one we've met before. Something has gone, something is missing. He gets up and we see him walk. He is still a physically commanding presence. Sits down with a newspaper. Younger player in whites – friendly, admiring - approaches him.

Tom?

Wills looks up.

Is that story true about you getting Geelong to kick the ball out of bounds every time they got it against Ballarat.

Too right, says Tom. They had the wind in the last quarter. Our boys kicked it out of the ground every time they got it. The miners rioted. We were two hours getting away from the ground.

Tom is amused. The younger player is impressed.

Sport's about winning, eh Tom?

Winning's the only thing. He turns at looks at the younger player with disarming frankness. What else is there in life? As far as I can see, there's nothing else.

Tom?

Yes.

"Let go the ball"

Goal in danger

You'll play with anyone, won't you?

Yes. If they pay me.

We're playing Melbourne today, Tom.

Yes.

Your old mates, Tom.

Yes.

Tom's not smiling any more.

We see the first ball of the match. Tommy bowls. The batsman is Tennant, the player he replaced as the captain of the Victorian XI. We see Tommy's bowling action, his approach to the crease. Over-arm bowling is now legal. His action is about contained power finding release at the moment of delivery. The ball jumps from a length striking Tennant in the elbow who drops his bat and cries out, smothering his cry as he does. He looks back at Wills, hatred in his eyes. Wills returns the glare. They don't like one another, never did, and out here on the sports field their animosity is naked.

38

1866, Lake Wallace, Western Victoria. A practice field. Tom Wills is playing cricket with a group of Aboriginal men while a group of squatters stand a short distance off watching with a local trooper called Kennedy and Gurnett, the tour promoter.

Gurnett: The plan is to take them to England.

Trooper: (shaking his head): They're not really cricketers. They just play now and then with the shearers.... .

Gurnett: They'll be fine. There's a new market in what's called "novelty entertainment". The All-England XI only came to Australia because

Charles Dickens couldn't come and do a reading tour - they packed out the MCG. The blacks will play cricket and then display their native skills during the breaks – throwing spears and boomerangs, dodging cricket balls flung at them with their shields. There's already interest in England and other colonies about them coming. And we've hired the best man to ready them for the job.

He points to Wills.

Squatter (enthusiastically): When he met them, he spoke to them in their lingo. The blacks are pretty good at hiding their feelings but he made a few heads turn when he did that, let me tell you.

Wills is assisting one of the Aboriginal players, Wattie, to find a bowling action, one that is more than coming in with his arm upheld and then jerking his arm at the moment of delivery.

Wills (in language): You throw spear this way.

He does the action with power and purpose and a grunt.

Wills (in English, holding up the ball): When you bowl ball - same.

He does a wrenching action with his body to indicate vigor and strength coming from his torso, through his shoulder, into his arm, finishing with the grunt of throwing a spear.

Garnett: The only problem with Wills is that he wants to take over. Where's he staying? Squatter (a bluff, beefy fellow, not terribly bright): My place. My wife is always complaining about my company. She can't wait to meet a Rugby and Cambridge man and have some decent conversation (laughs).

39

Colonial mansion. Dinner party. The squatter, his wife, their 10-year-old son, Wills. The wife, seriously bored by both her husband and the isolation of her existence, has a bright inquiring mind.

Wife: Mr Wills, my husband tells me you speak to the blacks in their language.

Wills: Yes, I learnt it as a child.

Wife: But surely you should be using English. Surely the purpose of teaching them cricket is to civilise them.

Wills: Is the game not civilized?

Wife taken aback.

Wife: Your father was murdered by blacks, was he not? How is it you can go amongst them and play games?

Wills. My father was murdered in Queensland.

She doesn't understand.

He continues: As they see the world, blaming them for a murder in Queensland is like blaming a group of Spaniards for a crime committed in Norway.

Wife: Is that how you see the issue?

He appears momentarily perplexed. Yes, yes, I think so.

She is a little taken aback by the abruptness of his replies. She tries again. Speaking to her husband, she says, Mr Wills was so kind as to give Lachlan an hour of his time before tea. They played cricket down by the shearing shed.

Johnny Mullagh, or Unaarrimin, the great player of the 1868 team that toured England.

Lachlan: Mr Wills showed me a better way to hold the bat. Mr Wills is captain of the Victorian XI and the Geelong Football Club. Last year, he was champion of the colony in football.

Father (laughing) Yes, yes, yes, Lachlan, I am well aware of Mr Wills' sporting credentials.

There is a moment of silence then, suddenly, Wills rises and says, in a formal way, bowing to the wife, Well, thank you for the meal. I have to go now – I have some business in Lake Wallace.

Bowing stiffly, he exits.

Wife: He is the opposite of what I expected. Had I not seen him play so beautifully with Lachlan, I would not have liked him at all.

40

Scene: Lake Wallace. Broad sheet of wintry water. Among some magnificent eucalypts at its edges, the black members of the cricket team sit around a fire. We see Wills approach them. The blacks look up, then one of them makes way for him – that is, as a member of the circle. Wills sits, opens a bottle of wine, takes a swig then passes it to the man on his left.

We realise we are watching this from the perspective of someone. We become aware it is Trooper Kennedy. Having witnessed this, he quietly absents himself from the scene. We see him walking back to his hut, opening the door and entering. A plain-looking woman who is his wife welcomes him into the orange warmth, saying, Here, you must be cold - come sit by the fire.

As he does so, we become aware that a young Aboriginal woman with a baby is sitting on the other side of the fire. It is clear that the residents of this house live together in some sort of harmony. The young Aboriginal woman may not be herself or feel herself at home but she is not in fear.

The baby coughs, the trooper's wife goes to the child, feels its brow, and says, "I think the fever is passing".

Trooper Kennedy: I saw something I did not wish to see tonight.

Wife (concerned by his tone of voice) What?

Kennedy: Young Mr Wills giving grog to the blacks.

41

Melbourne Cricket Ground Boxing Day 1866. We see the team forming for the famous portrait of the Australian Native XI, Wills in the middle of the back row, Mullagh on his left, Dick-a-Dick on the end of the front row. They are all neatly dressed, like waiters. None of them look particularly happy. Wills stands amid them, holding a bat. There is nothing which suggests he sees himself as being other than one of the team.

The camera moves back. We see that the photographer and the team are surrounded by a crowd – like the mounting yard at Flemington. The camera settles on the shoulder of a wealthily dressed man in his 60s with his expensively dressed wife. We hear his voice saying

They are a dying race. They'll soon be all gone. I've never seen one before.

The group being photographed break up just as a yob shouts, You're a dingo, Wills, playing with blacks after what they did to your father.

Wills, who is standing with the squatter, turns and looks at him: What was that?

The yob, less bravely, I said you were a dingo....

Wills is struck with the thought. He says to the squatter, My father poisoned all the dingoes on our station. The blacks had a dance for the dingo which they taught me. He's right – I'm a dingo.

Tom!

The Aboriginal Cricket team with Tom Wills at the Melbourne Cricket Ground 1866.

We see Sally struggling to get to the front of the crowd.

Sally! Tom moves towards her.

Tom, I read about your father's death in the newspapers. I didn't know how to contact you. I wanted to say I'm sorry.

Tom (stiffly) Thankyou.

The camera moves away and we see the hugeness of the day, the military band, the stalls, the wealthy members of society in their finery, the poor in their dirty ragged clothes, all among the gum trees in a place that still sees itself as a colony.

42

That night. Tom and Sally in bed, having made love. She is lying across his chest, as in the earlier scene.

What happened in Queensland, Tom?

It is a serious question, tenderly put.

I can't describe it. I have no words.

He pulls away from her, gets out of bed, crosses over to his coat, pulls out a whisky flask and has a swig. Then he stands listening.

In Queensland, of a night, I'd lie awake listening. The blacks, when they attack, don't use words. They agree upon the cry of a particular bird. So I'd be up there on my own and I'd hear a mopoke from out there (points). Then I'd hear another mopoke from over there (points in another direction, takes another swig). The terror would start swirling in my guts and I'd get my gun and wait for them to come.

He holds up his whisky flask. The only sleep I got was from this.

Sally: Come back to bed, Tom.

Tom Wills with his Aboriginal Cricket team at the MCG 1866.

He turns towards her. She takes off her top, he puts down the whisky flask, walks towards her and gets into bed. As they come face to face, she says

Don't worry about me wanting you to marry me, Tom. I'm already married.

He pulls back.

I left him a year ago and I'm not going back. He was violent.

Tom looks at her, sees she means what she says and that her tenderness towards him is undiminished and welcomes her embrace. Then he stops and says.

It's funny but I feel safe when I'm with the blacks in the cricket team.

43

Geelong, January 1867. A house at Point Henry on the edge of Geelong, home of Elizabeth Wills. It is a timber construction and while adequate does not have the grandeur of her previous home outside Ararat. Three of Tom's young sisters is home with her. We see the entrance to the property, the long drive, trees hedging one side. In to it turns a dray with Tom and the 10 Aboriginal cricketers, slowly making its plodding way up the drive. A young girl, Tom's sister, looks out and is shocked by what she sees.

She cries out: M-mother

Elizabeth appears. The strain of having held the family together after Horatio's death is evident in her face.

Daughter. Mother, it's Tom! He's – he's – brought Aborigines with him!

Elizabeth rushes to the window, throws a hand to her mouth to stifle her cry. Both mother and daughter back away from the window, unknowing of what to do. There is a knock at the front door. Elizabeth composes herself. She has been through many challenges – this is another one she must rise to meet. We see her courage but she is also unsettled. We see from behind her as she opens the door. There's Tom – behind and around him are the Aboriginal players.

Mother, he says brightly, my team-mates. We played in Geelong yesterday so I thought today I would treat them to one of your afternoon teas.

Multiple emotions register on her face. Then she says, Of course, come in.

44

Inside the house. The players, in their waiters' uniforms, sit in line with cups of tea in their hands. Tom's manner is bright and gay. This is the happiest we will see him in the period between the massacre and his death. He is sitting in the middle of the blacks, telling his mother and sisters, about the forthcoming tour of England. He's raving.

We're going to England, he's saying. We're going to play the MCC at Lord's. What's more, we'll win. We're getting better with every game. We crushed Corio yesterday. The lads stand fearless before the fastest ball. This is the opportunity I've been looking for mother.

We see Elizabeth's face. She looks at the Aborigines. For them, this situation is weird but their reality is permanently weird. They've lost their families, their lands, their ceremonies, their sacred places. They exist as novelty entertainments. Elizabeth finds herself staring at Dick-a-dick. He puts down his cup of tea and says, Thank you, missus. His face says he knows just how weird this scene is.

Tom (excitedly) In the breaks, Dick-a-Dick here stands with his traditional shield and invites young men standing 15 yards away to hit him with a cricket ball. They never get him. He taunts them. Tell mother what you say.

The face of Dick-a-Dick, to be played by Ernie Dingo, splits into a grin, "I say, "You not tryin'"

Tom laughs loudly, excited by the joke.

Wattie, a small polite man, says, One of the whitefellers at the MCG say, "Wills – he talk to you in English". I say, "Wills no use. He along us. He talk blackfeller language".

This got a big laugh at the MCG but not from Tom's mother.

Elizabeth: You will be some making money from the enterprise, won't you Tom? I never go into Geelong that I'm not confronted by one of your creditors.

Oh yes, mother. The tour is being run by Mr Gurnett. He's a crook. I'm going to take it over. There's going to be big money in this for me.

Elizabeth (disbelievingly): Is there Tom?

45

An hour or so later. Elizabeth and her daughters stand on the verandah, waving off Tom and the team. He's still full of beans and judges the visit to be a great success. The cart plods off down the drive with them all aboard. Elizabeth watches them go and says.

This land is cursed. It is split between black and white in a way which will never heal. My son is a child standing in the middle, playing games, and the one person who might have saved him, his father, is dead, robbed from me –

She turns, tearful, and walks away.

46

Rainy night. The wagon carrying the Aboriginal cricketers and the squatter is returning to Lake Wallace. They stop outside the house of the trooper, the men slowly and miserably alight, their bodies cold and wet through. A body wrapped in a blanket is seen in the back of the wagon.

1. Mr. G. Smith
2. Tiger
3. Dick-a-Dick
4. Mosquito

9. Cozens
10. Henry Rose
11. Bullocky
12. Jim Crow

5. King Cole
6. Mullagh
7. Lawrence (Capt.)
8. Redcap

13. Peter
14. Twopenny
15. Sundown
16. Mr. W. R. Hayman

The Aboriginal Cricket team as photographed by Patrick Dawson in Hamilton Victoria, prior to their 1868 Tour of England.

The squatter goes and knocks on the door of the hut. The trooper appears, surprised at being called out at this time of night on such an evening. In the orange light behind him we see his wife, the young Aboriginal mother and the child.

Squatter: One of the native cricketers died half a day back. His body's in the cart.

Trooper grabs a lamp, walks out into the rain, sees the body in the blanket.

Trooper: Which one?

Squatter: Wattie. What he died of I can't say but he'd been drinking all through the tour. Two others are also dead, Jellico and Sugar.

Trooper: Was alcohol involved in each case?

Squatter: I'm afraid so.

Trooper: How did they procure the alcohol?

Squatter: Hard to say.

Trooper: Did you see young Mr Wills among them with grog?

Squatter: Once or twice...

Trooper (looking at the body of Wattie and the back at the squatter): Can you imagine what is going to happen to the rest of them (pointing to the other members of the team) if Wills goes with them to England? Can you see this lot in the back streets of London after he's got pissed and passed out in some East End dive? I'm going to make it my business to see that Wills does not go on that tour.

47

1873, Kadina, South Australia. A coach pulls up outside a pub in the middle of what looks a lot like nowhere. Flat, pink, stony, infernally hot. A

(Top) Tom Wills as he played for Victoria in 1868; (lower)
WG Grace as he was in Victoria 1873.

massive bearded figure is first from the coach. It's 25-year-old WG Grace, the young king of English cricket in the early years of his long reign. He takes a look at the landscape which is smouldering in the midday heat. An Englishman appears beside him and immediately squints.

Englishman: Christ! This looks like another planet. They better be paying us a lot of money to play out here, Grace.

Grace: They are and you will get your share. I better go and have a look at the playing field, if that indeed is what it is.

The rest of the team slowly emerges from the coach as Grace walks away. A kid appears on a bike. Riding flat-out past Grace, he says: Hey Fatso! We're going to beat you! We've got Tom Wills on our team.

Grace stops. Turns and calls to his team-mates.

Mister Wills is playing for the home team.

Englishman. That's hardly surprising. He's played for every other team we've met.

48

Dark hotel room, Tom's hotel room. We see Tom, awoken by the noise outside in the street. He pulls his body out of bed. We see an empty whisky bottle on the table beside the bed. He is hungover but we also see how stiff and sore he is. Just walking is hard for him. He's 37 years old. He's been drinking for 20 years. He opens the curtain, sees that Grace and the team have arrived, lurches back towards the chair. We see him, with difficulty, get into his whites, then he dresses. We see him do a few exercises to get himself moving ever so slightly, then he sets forth, passing country people, miners, their families.

We hear voices complimenting Tom. "Give it to the Poms, Tommy". He winks at his supporters, another he gives the old thumbs up, but we can see that he is limping slightly.

49

WG Grace stands in whites, cap and club coat surveying the playing field. Tom appears. They walk together to the centre of the field, stones crunching beneath their feet. Tom is still limping slightly.

Grace: Tom, why do you keep playing?

Tom: I can't stop playing games. That's what my father always said of me – Tom can't stop playing games. (He nods agreeably). And I have a few debts.

Grace: We're playing in Adelaide tomorrow.

Tom: That puts you in breach of your contract with the people here. This is to be your only game in South Australia.

Grace, Yes, well…..

Tom (humorously): Yes, well, that's one of those agreements us gentlemen make, eh Grace?.

Tom tosses a coin, Grace calls heads. Heads it is.

Grace: You can have a bat, Tom.

50

Tom goes out to bat. We see him leave the bush pavilion. We see the locals pat him on his way. Tom still has all the mannerisms of a master batsman. He stills hears the crowd, still responds to their call. He takes the wicket with a look of command, surveying the field. The English

Tom Wills by William Handcock, Melbourne 1870.

bowler is young and quick and his first ball is through Tom before he sees it, flattening his stumps.

We see the delivery from the pavilion, hear the collective Hmph! of air as the confidence is taken out of the home side. Their champion has gone first ball. We see in quick succession, one, two, three wickets. We see a sign saying York Peninsula All Out 24. Then we see one saying Grace XI 0/85, 1/160, Grace 56 not out. We see the bush pavilion is now half-empty.

Tommy's bowling spin. Grace strokes him to the midfield boundary. He advances and hits him out of the ground. Third ball the camera slows down Tommy's action, we see how he puts everything into the delivery, all his strength, all his guile, finishing with a grunt, the same grunt he gave Watty showing him how bowling a cricket ball was like throwing a spear. We see the ball hovering through the air, spinning in flight. We see Grace's eyes taken in. We see the ball land and spin quickly off the pitch, between Grace's bat and pad and into his stumps.

Yes! cries Tommy, clutching at air like his fist is an eagle's talon. Turning to Grace he says with a grin, That's why I keep on playing, Grace. I like sending cocky bastards like you back to the pavilion.

51

Geelong 1874. Tommy's last game of football. We see him going down in the middle of a pack pretending to be hit. It's an old stager's trick. He gets up holding his eye, complaining to the umpire that he didn't get a free kick and pointing to his much younger opponent, saying, "He hit me!". The umpire waves him away. Tommy returns to his position in front of goal. Opponent stands beside him.

Opponent: I didn't hit you.

Tom: Of course you didn't. You're a gentleman. You go to a gentleman's school.

Opponent: Yes.

Tom: I went to one of them once over there in England. Buggery going on everywhere.

Opponent: No!

Tom: Yes! So don't come too close, mate, you never know where I've been.

Opponent stands off. Ball comes downfield and finds Tom alone. Thanks, he says. He goes back – stylishly – takes his time, goals and is clearly impressed by what he has done, smacking his fist. Stands back on his opponent.

Tom: Don't worry. This is my last game.

Opponent: I won't be sorry to see you go.

Tom: Oh, I'm not going. I'm going to become an umpire.

Opponent: But you break all the rules.

Tom: When you make the rules, you can break the rules. And that's not all. I've become an ambassador for the Geelong Football Club.

52

Adelaide, February 1879. Room full of football delegates from around Australia. Tom is reading a speech. He is a drunk, a dreamer but he is also a founder of the game – and he is being listened to. Already they know the game they've invented is phenomenally popular. Victoria has its own Football Association, there has already been a night game at the MCG:

James Smith Pearce, Kapunda footballer, Adelaide 1879.

Tom: This is an age of innovation. This is the time to take our game to Britain and America. Everywhere our game goes, it works, everywhere it goes, it excites crowds and supporters. It's in all the southern states of Australia, it's in Queensland and New Zealand. We should by-pass Sydney and go to the world. It is the king of games. Soccer does not use the hands. Rugby is trench warfare and has too many injuries. Our game is swift and open. Players can leap to catch the ball. I can speak on behalf of the Geelong Football Club. My cousin Colden Harrison can speak on behalf of the Melbourne club. My proposal is that we send both clubs to Britain and ask to play the football clubs of that country. We will play their game if they will play ours. Then may be it a case of let the best code win. But if we don't go now it will be too late. Soccer is called the simple game for a reason, and that is why it is spreading. Rugby is only seven years old as code but it appeals to the military minded. Our game appeals to those who love seeing young men fly in the air and brave it in the packs and kick the ball long ways accurately -

South Australian delegate: I'm with you. Tom! South Australia will support you if you can get the support of the Victorian Football Association.

Tom (cocky): They'll listen to me, alright. I invented the bloody game.

Loud round of support for Tom

53

Meeting of Victorian Football Association. We recognise JB Ellis and William Tennant, Wills' old foes. Tom is reading the same speech but the reception is entirely different. No-one is listening, or not in a way that suggests belief. Tennant shakes his head and looks away

Tom is partly drunk but still making sense: This is an age of innovation. This is the time to take our game to Britain and America otherwise we will see that in one hundred years' time Australian football will remain isolated in Australia......

GRAND MILITARY FOOTBALL MATCH
By
ELECTRIC LIGHT.
PROFESSOR PEPPER.
Will give an **EXHIBITION**
Of the
ELECTRIC LIGHT,
On the Melbourne Cricket-ground,
TUESDAY EVENING, 5th AUGUST,
When a Grand Military Football Match will be
played.
Particulars in future advertisements.

(Top) August 5 1879 advertisement. (lower); the first football match at the MCG under electric lighting August 30 1879.

Tom finishes and looks up.

President (trying to be kind): Thank you, Tom. We will consider your proposal and advise you of our decision.

Tom: You don't want – to discuss it? In Adelaide, it was carried by acclamation.

President (holding up a piece of paper): We've got a very full agenda, Tom. But I assure you, you will hear from us within the month.

Tom looks round the faces, sees the disinterest of some like Tennant. Others can't look him in the eyes.

Tom: This is a brush-off

President: No, Tom, we invited you in to deliver your speech. We will now think upon what you have said but I'm afraid that does have to be the end of the discussion for tonight.

Tom stands. About to leave the room, he turns and says (quietly, hoarsely): None of you ever had my (pointing to himself) my vision

Makes an unsteady exit, shutting door behind him.

They are all grateful to see the end of him.

Tennant: Did you hear what he said at the Adelaide meeting? He said he invented the game.

Tennant laughs at the idea.

Ellis: We had to sack him after eight months as secretary of the Melbourne Cricket Club. The place was a total mess. He'd done nothing practical, there was money missing.

Tennant: People don't want to say it because he's the great Tom Wills but he's a drunk who was a cheat and a bully on the sports field. He wanted the football code that most resembled him as a player because that way he

had the best chance of winning. His selfishness was epic. He had supporters in the press who cheered him on and the result is the poor, deluded
fool we saw tonight. We are running a football association that is struggling to pay its ground dues and he wants to send two teams to England!
Let's put it to the vote.

President: Those for?

No hands are raised.

Those against?

All the hands go up.

54

Tom pushing through the front door of the cottage in Heidelberg – then
a rural village outside Melbourne - he shares with Sally. Drunker than
at the meeting but stable. Goes straight to cupboard, pulls out whisky
bottle, takes two gulps.

Sally (worried): Tom – should you be drinking like that?

Tom takes two more swigs.

Sally: Tom – please don't – the doctor warned you –

He takes two more swigs. He is on his way to getting horribly drunk even
by his standards. He turns and faces her and hisses with quiet fury: The
game is over!!!

55

Five hours later, Sally is shaken awake. It's Tom. He's mad. He has one
hand over her mouth.

Quiet, he's saying, quiet. I heard a mopoke out there. If we hear another one, it could be them, they could be coming with their spears and waddies. I'll fight for my life, they'll throw a spear. It'll bring me down like a kangaroo. Then they'll club me about the head to kill me. That's how they fight up here.

His terrified eyes are scanning the horizon.

56

Next morning, Sally is having breakfast. Tom appears, dressed in a black suit. He sits opposite her.

Sally: Why are you dressed up, Tom.

Tom: Off to church, off to church. Got to say goodbye. (He looks at her). I'm going. There's no place for me here, never was. (He frowns at the thought – then, looking back at Sally) . Do you want to come, too?

Sally: Go where, Tom?

Tom: To die. I'm going to kill myself.

We see Sally's fear.

57

Sally in her front yard with a basket. Tom walking in circle saying, I need to go to church and pray. Our Father Who Art in Heaven. (He throws himself wholly into the prayer then falls backwards a step, saying to the heavens). I failed my Father who is in Heaven.

Sally hands the basket over the fence to her neighbour, a similarly aged woman. The neighbour rolls back the kitchen towel covering the basket and sees it's full of knives.

Sally: Thank you for this – I've removed every sharp knife in the house so he can't harm himself.

Sally hurries back to the house. Goes inside the. Tom passes behind her, saying, There is only one course for a man like me.

He is clearly looking for something. We see him sight a pair of scissors. He grabs them and pushing out his left arm to bar Sally grabbing him or the scissors, he stabs himself in the heart rather like a Roman committing suicide. Sally struggles with him, crying out, No, Tom, no. He pulls out the scissors and in the course of sinking to his knees, strikes himself again.

Sally (weeping): Why, Jesus? Jesus, why?

58

Burial scene. Heidelberg cemetery. 8 am. Five people, one of them the gravedigger, stand beside an open grave that is in the process of being filled. The two closest to us we recognise from the meeting of the Victorian Football Association.

Committeeman: Where is the woman who lived with him?

President: She wasn't told the hour of burial in case she made a scene. The family are going to pay her to stay away.

Committeeman: Is there to be a memorial?

President: No. His mother believes he is damned. She has asked that his name never be mentioned in her presence again.

The grave digger finishes, smooths the dirt, pats it down with his boots. The pair stare at the place where the famous Tom Wills is to lie.

President: It's to be an unmarked grave.

*(Top) Sherrin's first advertisement for their sporting goods
1880. (lower); Tom Will's grave at Heidelberg Cemetry.
Originally unmarked, this memorial was added in the 1960s.*

He shrugs and turns, the other committeemen walking with him to a horse and carriage 50 metres away on the brow of the hill.

The camera stays where it is behind the two men. At a certain point the camera freezes on the two committeemen, the horse and cart, the bare hill and that is when it starts, an Irish lament played on the Irish pipes and by that instrument alone. Not a jig, not a reel, but one of those grand Irish tunes that open to the immense sadness and loneliness of the human condition with all that accompanies us being the solitary spirit captured in the song.

The frozen scene of the committeemen fades into darkness. These words appear.

In June 1868, the Australian Native XI led the M.C.C. on the first innings. If Tom Wills had played, they might well have won, making him the first Australian captain to win at Lord's.

That screen darkens. The Irish pipes fade. They are replaced with the sound of an AFL telecast. Melbourne v Port Adelaide 2010. We hear the build-up, the excitement in the commentator's voice. Then we see it - Liam Jurrah's Mark of the Year.

http://www.youtube.com/watch?v=NF-_HszEC9s

We see it not just from one angle, but two, but three. We hear the cries of JUUUURRRRAAAAAHH!!!! This is Australian football at its best. More clips, more excitement, then the MCG on grand final day from overhead, people drawing in thousands towards the ground, painted faces. Sydney v Hawks would be a good one.

Freeze. Darken. The following words appear.

"Today AFL is Australia's most popular spectator sport. But Tom Wills was right. Its best chance of becoming as truly global game was in the 1880s and '90s."

Credits start to appear and one of 3 songs.

Either Mick Thomas ("Weddings, Parties, Anything") or Shane Howard ("Goanna"). Both have happy-go-lucky Tom Wills songs that go back to the spirit of Tom as he was when he arrived back in Melbourne of 1856 and revolutionised Victorian sport

http://www.myspace.com/mickthomassongs/music/songs/tom-wills-37957983

http://www.youtube.com/watch?v=NqcAD15N-aA (shane howard)

OR

Neil Murray ("Warumpi Band") "Tom Wills Would" – a serious character study of TWW by someone who understands his solitary path better than most. Neil grew up in Tjapwurrung country, speaks an Aboriginal language, has Aboriginal kids.

http://www.youtube.com/watch?v=SCUm2IZMrbc

THE END

Statue of Tom Wills refereeing the first Australian Rules football match in 1858 between Melbourne Grammar and Scotch College, outside the Melbourne Cricket Ground.

www.ingramcontent.com/pod-product-compliance
Lightning Source LLC
Chambersburg PA
CBHW020907100426
42737CB00044B/660